My Brilliant Brain: A Practical Resource for Understanding Anxiety and Implementing Self-Calming

This resource uses simple yet effective shared language for adults and children, allowing them to talk about anxiety, and taking away the shame and blame that children may experience in response to these emotions. It encourages sharing, allowing the feelings of worry and anxiety to become normalised and the child to feel more in control.

Full of activities and experiential learning for individual children, groups or classes, this guide covers topics such as:

- The brain, the amygdala, what anxiety is and how it is normal.
- Demonstrating and modelling calm, even if you are not, to help reassure and protect the children under your care.
- Self-calming activities and strategies.
- Being a Child in Charge – helping children to develop individual strategies that work best for them.

Designed for use alongside the storybook *Myg and Me: Understanding Anxiety and Implementing Self-Calming*, teachers, support staff, therapists and parents will find this guidebook an indispensable tool in the process of helping the children they interact with to feel a sense of self-determination and self-efficacy.

Liz Bates is an independent education consultant. She supports both primary and secondary schools in all aspects of Emotional Health and Wellbeing, and Safeguarding, including whole school approaches, training staff and delivering talks to parents. Liz is a Protective Behaviours Trainer, a Wellbeing Award Advisor for Optimus and a regular contributor at national conferences.

W0112684

My Brilliant Brain: A Practical Resource for Understanding Anxiety and Implementing Self-Calming

LIZ BATES
ILLUSTRATED BY NIGEL DODDS

Routledge
Taylor & Francis Group
LONDON AND NEW YORK

First published 2022
by Routledge
2 Park Square, Milton Park, Abingdon, Oxon OX14 4RN

and by Routledge
605 Third Avenue, New York, NY 10158

Routledge is an imprint of the Taylor & Francis Group, an informa business

© 2022 Liz Bates and Nigel Dodds

The right of Liz Bates and Nigel Dodds to be identified as authors of this work has been asserted in accordance with sections 77 and 78 of the Copyright, Designs and Patents Act 1988.

All rights reserved. The purchase of this copyright material confers the right on the purchasing institution to photocopy pages which bear the photocopy icon and copyright line at the bottom of the page. No other parts of this book may be reprinted or reproduced or utilised in any form or by any electronic, mechanical, or other means, now known or hereafter invented, including photocopying and recording, or in any information storage or retrieval system, without permission in writing from the publishers.

Trademark notice: Product or corporate names may be trademarks or registered trademarks, and are used only for identification and explanation without intent to infringe.

British Library Cataloguing-in-Publication Data
A catalogue record for this book is available from the British Library

Library of Congress Cataloging-in-Publication Data
A catalog record has been requested for this book

ISBN: 978-1-032-06907-4 (pbk)
ISBN: 978-1-003-20445-9 (ebk)

DOI: 10.4324/9781003204459

Typeset in Zag
by codeMantra

Contents

Introduction

Welcome to *My Brilliant Brain*, the accompanying resource for the children's storybook *Myg and Me*.

It may be that you work mainly with children who are significantly anxious or perhaps you work with groups or classes of children whose experiences and feelings cover a wider range of levels of worry or anxiety. Or possibly you live with a child who is struggling at the moment. Whichever child or children you work or live with, I hope you will find something in this resource to make their lives feel a little more manageable, for them to feel a little more in control. And maybe you too will find a way to manage an anxiety, because it happens to us all.

There are many reasons why children and young people may become anxious at school or at home. If that anxiety is preventing a child from accessing learning or doing the things they want or need to do then it is important that the child is helped to manage and overcome those, often, paralysing feelings. The storybook and resource are designed to give children strategies to use but also to pre-empt the feeling of overwhelm by teaching them *about* anxiety – where it comes from, why it happens and, most importantly, that it happens to everyone, that it is ok and that a lot of the time we can manage it. Giving children the understanding and the strategies to manage anxiety and to self-calm is to give them a crucial skill set.

At times of anxiety and fear the activity of the amygdala – part of the survival brain – can override the pre-frontal cortex, the thinking brain. If we want children to be able to think, plan, organise, co-operate, negotiate and learn then we need to help them to achieve the sense of safety that is required by the brain in order for this to take place.

So meet Myg, the main character of the children's storybook. If you haven't guessed already, Myg is the a**myg**dala. The book explains, simply and charmingly, about the amygdala. That Myg has always been there; that Myg looks out for me; that Myg helps to keep me safe; that Myg powers up my legs to run from a crocodile, or gives me the strength to tackle aliens; but that sometimes Myg works too hard – so a school test or a diving board become 'monsters' that I should fight, run away from, or freeze to the spot to avoid. And that is when I have to become a 'Child in Charge'.

DOI: 10.4324/9781003204459-1

This adult resource takes six sessions with explanations, a quiz, discussions and activities, to work through with a certificate at the end, covering:

- My brilliant brain – finding out about my brain
- Meet Myg – a bit more about the brain
- This happens to everyone – anxiety is 'normal'
- Where is my brilliant brain? – what happens to my brain when I am anxious?
- Lots of ways to help – a wide variety of self-calming activities and strategies, using all of the senses
- Being a Child in Charge – creating an individual set of strategy cards for each child – what works for them.

As you look through each session, you will see that they may vary in length when delivered. Some discussions and activities may take longer than others depending on the contributions the children make. Session 5 in particular may be spread over a number of lessons/meetings/days.

Their calmness starts with you

Never in the history of calming down has anyone ever calmed down by being *told* to 'calm down!'

It will not help and will not stop the anxiety if we tell an anxious child that there is nothing to worry about, that there is no need to get upset or angry and not to make a fuss. Because for them there is something to worry about, they have a reason to be upset and their 'making a fuss' is likely to be something over which they have no control. We do not know their lived experience and their upset or anger is likely to be their way of telling us something. It is important to validate their feelings and what is happening:

> 'I can see that you are feeling …'
>
> 'I understand why you are …'
>
> 'How can I help you?'
>
> 'This is a big feeling, but it will pass …'

rather than shut them down, and we have to wait until the amygdala is no longer in control before we attempt to rationalise with an anxious child. Teaching the strategies described later in this resource cannot be done while the amygdala is in charge – we teach them at a calm time. So, when a child *is* experiencing anxiety they will then have some strategies, already learned, to call on.

Demonstrating and modelling calm, even if you are not, is an important skill for a parent or an adult working with children. Children are aware when others around them are anxious. They understand if they should feel anxious by watching others around them, and seeing anxiety in adults will feel unsafe for them. An anxious adult looks like they are not managing and so cannot be a protector. Having a measured response, even if you are feeling anxious on the inside, can help a child. Your calmness will help to reassure them.

This resource uses a simple yet effective shared language for adults and children to talk about anxiety (Myg). By making anxiety a creature it takes away shame and blame that children may experience in response to these emotions, and makes the feeling 'normal', shared, and the child more in control.

This is a self-reflection which I invite you to try and to share with your colleagues before using the resource with children.

Self-reflection

Take a moment to reflect:

- What type of interactions/events would lead to anxiety for you?
- How do you respond emotionally, mentally and physically when anxious?
- What do you do to manage or control your anxieties?
- How do you control your emotions, thoughts, physical responses? Can you? Do you?
- How do you know what to do?
- Are there situations you wish you had managed differently/'better'?
- Did anyone ever help by telling you to calm down? Or did they help you to calm down?
- There's a difference.
- What support do you use? Do you have support?
- How do you know what support there is for you? And how do you access it?

That reflection may have helped you to think about how you approach your own anxiety; what do you do, does it help, and how do you know what to do? Did someone teach you or did you work it out through trial and error? Perhaps you are not always very successful and would like to manage it better. Or maybe you have some amazing strategies which you use effectively. If you are a teacher then you will know, hopefully, how to control your anxieties in front of a new class. The point is you may know now what to do, but did you know as an eight-year-old child?

Using this resource means you will be taking responsibility for your own feelings. It is important to avoid an 'us and them' approach (adults are sensible and strong, children are anxious and misbehave); if you can reflect on your own experiences of anxiety it increases empathy and understanding. Calming and regulation can often be a reciprocal relationship.

Your experience is key – we can pass on our skills to children – but more importantly your understanding and management of your own anxieties will enable you to support children more effectively.

And if you feel you could use a bit more help, the strategies in Session 5 later in this resource work just as well for adults as they do for children, so you may want to make your own set of strategy cards.

The brain

This is not a biology textbook, but it is important to understand the part the brain plays in the evolution of anxiety.

Anxiety occurs when our perceived capacity to cope is surpassed by what we have to deal with and we fear failure, harm, humiliation, the unknown, the known. We all experience anxiety at times – but we may experience it differently and about different things. Some of us love rollercoasters, some of us hate them.

It is a natural physiological response to threat, uncertainty, fear, and its roots are to be found in the part of the brain called the amygdala. This is the centre of our emotional responses and it is one of the oldest parts of the brain – designed to keep us alive, designed to send messages to our brain, to power up our body, to react in the face of threat. You will know this as fight/flight (and freeze, and there are more), and this will be covered later in this resource. So we certainly don't want our brains to stop doing this – it is a life-saving response – but there are times when the perceived threat may not be as potentially dangerous as our brains first think. It is at this point that we can employ self-calming and self-regulating strategies to help us to manage a situation. And the reason why it is important to do this is because when our amygdala is in charge, our pre-frontal cortex – our thinking brain – is compromised.

Imagine crossing the road and seeing a lorry heading for you. Without thinking you run to the side of the road. *Without thinking.* That's the important bit. You don't want to be thinking 'I wonder how fast that lorry is travelling' or ' Shall I run, or jog or just walk a bit faster?' because by then it will be too late. However, do you remember ever sitting in an exam and, in the first few moments of anxiety, forgetting everything you have learnt? That is the point at which you took charge and calmed yourself, took a few deep breaths, and then your thinking brain got going again.

Helping children to understand that this is a common feeling, experienced by everyone, is the first step in giving them the skills and strategies to self-calm. They are not weird or unusual or silly or weak or pathetic to feel like this. Anxiety drives anxiety, so if a child feels there is something wrong with them because they feel anxious, then that has the potential to increase their anxiety. Ask an astronaut, a fire-fighter, a free climber and they will have strategies they use to manage their fears and anxieties – be it breathing, visualisation, positive self-talk or something else.

Most of us live with and manage our anxieties. It can become a problem if the anxiety is actually preventing me from living my life the way I want to or need to. If it prevents me from doing the things I want to do.And it is exactly the same for a child or young person. Are their worries stopping them from learning, joining in, having a go, trying things out, taking those everyday risks that are inherent in learning?

Anxiety

How does it feel?

This will be covered later in the resource, but briefly all the feelings associated with anxiety come from natural, physiological responses to real or perceived threat (the brain doesn't know the difference). They come from the amygdala sending messages to prepare the body to react to that threat – to fight, to run or to freeze. The heart beating fast, the gulping breaths, the sick feeling, wanting to go to the toilet, the sweating and so on. When you get to Session 2 all the explanation will be there, importantly, to share with and explain to the children.

How does it look?

If we continue with the understanding that this is a response from our amygdala to threat, then anxiety can look like fight, flight or freeze.

It may look like:

Fight

- Aggression
- The need to control – not to dominate but to protect
- Loud voice
- Tense muscles
- Balling fists
- Increasing height

Flight

- Escape
- Hiding
- Avoidance
- Restlessness
- Pacing
- Jitteriness

Freeze

- Switching off
- Shutting down
- Loss of concentration

- Losing focus
- Loss of understanding

And emotions – anger, tears. Because it is about big emotions, we may see big anger and big tears. We have to remember that all behaviour makes sense at the time. When anxiety is driving the behaviour, it is because the brain has registered a threat or lack of safety. It has nothing to do with what is actually threatening or unsafe but everything to do with what the brain perceives as such and these anxieties or fears may have their roots in events that happened in our childhoods which we may not even consciously remember.

Another example is our fertile imaginations and our ability to 'predict' the future – correctly or otherwise. Take flying.

Flying is statistically the safest way to travel and yet there are probably far more people who have a fear of flying than a fear of travelling by car.

That doesn't make sense – but then anxiety is not about making sense - it doesn't always make sense. It may be difficult to understand someone's fear of flying if we don't have that fear ourselves and this can lead to misunderstanding, misreading and dismissing another person's behaviours.

How often might we misunderstand these signs and behaviours in the children we work with? By understanding what anxiety is and where it comes from, we can help children to make sense of what is happening to them and then manage this if they need to.

How does it sound?

We all have a voice in our head. Our thoughts. A worry is a thought, not necessarily a fact.

Sometimes we say our thoughts out loud and give voice to our anxieties, and sometimes we keep them hidden inside our heads. Such as…

I can't

I'm rubbish

I don't know

I hate this

You don't understand

And many, many more. In Session 5, you will find much more on this as well as alternatives that we can give to children, to change that inner (and sometimes 'out-loud') voice.

In Session 4, there is a highlighted section for you with more detail about responding to a child who may be in fight, flight or freeze. Things to say and things to do.

Learning

We know that anxiety can both limit and prevent learning and achievement.

A child may:

- Worry about making mistakes and taking risks.
- Focus on what they 'can't do'.
- Be cautious of trying new things.
- Avoid mistakes by avoiding situations.
- Complain of physical ailments rather than engage in an unfamiliar activity.

Or

- Maintain a self-fulfilling prophecy of inadequacy.
- Seek negative attention to avoid a task.
- Have increased levels of low self-esteem.
- Exploit work avoidance techniques.

And it is also possible that adults may eventually give up and:

- Expect less of them.
- Leave them to fail.

Perhaps the most important thing we can do to help children is to normalise anxiety.

Anxiety is an ally. It is there for a reason – it is there to look after you.

It is there to alert you to danger. Sometimes the danger is real and sometimes the danger is in our heads. Whichever it is, the brain sees it as something to be dealt with – to fight it, to run away from it and so on.

So the feelings that come with anxiety is our bodies getting ready to do just that.

Format

Throughout the resource, the following are used:

- Plain text indicates information and descriptions of the process for you, the adult.
- *Italic text is used for verbatim instructions, questions, guidance and explanations. You can read/speak these directly to the children if you wish.*

So meet Myg and begin the process of helping the children you work with, or live with, to feel a sense of self-determination and self-efficacy. Help them to understand that they can be in control of their feelings, their thoughts and their actions, and that they do not have to be controlled and limited by their fears and anxieties.

Liz Bates
lizslamer@gmail.com

Session 1
My Brilliant Brain

Finding out about my brain

The Key Stage 1 and Key Stage 2 Science curriculum will have introduced children to some concepts that can be related to the brain.

Key Stage 1

Naming parts of the body – children will have named 'the head'.

Your brain sits inside your head.

Animals have basic needs for survival – water, food, air.

The brain tells you when you are thirsty and hungry and controls your lungs so that you breathe.

Key Stage 2

Humans have skeletons – the skull is part of the skeleton.

Your brain sits inside your skull.

Light helps us to see.

Your eyes are part of your brain.

Human development to old age.

Your brain began to grow 16 days after fertilisation.

Your growth and development are controlled by your brain.

DOI: 10.4324/9781003204459-2

Everything that makes you who you are is controlled by your brain.

It may be helpful to recap on this learning.

Read pages 1 and 2 of the storybook *Myg and Me*.

Discussion – My brilliant brain

Use all the questions from pages 1 and 2 in the storybook as discussion starters.

What do you think your brain helps you to do?

Bring in all the senses, too, such as:

- My brain enables me to feel my dog's fur when I stroke her.
- My brain enables me to see my friend's smiling face.
- My brain enables me to hear my favourite singer/band.
- My brain enables me to smell the fish and chips my dad brings home.
- My brain enables me to taste hot chillis, ice cream and strawberry laces.

On the IWB (interactive white board), write the following sentence:

Th nxt qstn s nmbr fv; wrt tht nmbr n yr bk.

Can anyone work out what that sentence is?

The sentence is:

The next question is number five; write that number in your book.

Our brilliant brains can even read a sentence when some of the letters are missing.

With some children, you may want to use a simpler approach:

What are these animals?

ct dg pg cw tgr cml lphnt

Our brilliant brains can even read words when some of the letters are missing.

Activity – My brilliant brain (Appendix 1)

In the brain outline, draw pictures or write lots of examples of what your brilliant brain can do.

Invite the children to talk about what is in their brain picture.

Activity – Facts and fibs (Appendix 2)

Children can have a set of questions and work through the facts and fibs individually, in pairs or in small groups – sharing responsibility for the answers, deciding which is a fact and which is a fib.

When all groups have answered, they can then share with the whole class.

Using **Appendix 3,** you can then give them the correct answers – reinforcing just how brilliant our brains are.

You could extend this activity by setting a research project to find out more detail about the facts and the true answers for the fibs. Or for the children to find out more facts about the brain.

Activity – Where in the brain? (Appendix 4)

The brain outline shows that different areas of the brain are responsible for different reactions and responses.

This is a rough diagram, but gives an idea of where certain areas are located – not just on the outer surface but within the brain.

Please note that, although our eyes are at the front of our heads, the part of the brain responsible for vision is located at the back.

A project folder for *Myg and Me* or *My Brilliant Brain* can be started for all their activity sheets and any other supporting work.

Session 2
Meet Myg

A bit more about the brain

Read pages 3–8 of the storybook *Myg and Me*.

Activity – Where's Myg? (using Appendix 4)

So we know that 'Myg' is short for 'amygdala'.

We know that it is a very special part of our brain.

Have a guess – where in the brain is Myg the amygdala?

Children can draw a tiny Myg on **Appendix 4** showing where they think the amygdala might be.

You can then show them **(Appendix 5)** and explain that the amygdala is deep inside the brain not on the surface.

A lot of the time Myg is laid-back, watching the world go by, but the reason that Myg is so important is because it leaps into action by spotting where there is danger and helps to keep us safe by responding to danger.

So what does Myg do?

DOI: 10.4324/9781003204459-3

Read pages 9–12 of the storybook *Myg and Me*.

The amygdala 'wakes up' when it thinks there might be danger. This is a very important job because it can help us in an emergency. It gets us ready to fight an alien, to run away from a crocodile or even to play dead if a big purple hairy monster is looking through our windows. But even though we don't live surrounded by crocodiles or other wild animals or weird creatures, our amygdala is ready to protect us from the dangers we might actually meet. Imagine crossing the road and then suddenly a lorry comes around the corner heading for you ... You'd run as fast as you could to the side of the road ... without even thinking about it. That's because your amygdala is in charge. It gives you the strength and the speed to run by sending messages to the rest of your brain and all around your body.

So Myg is great at getting our bodies ready when there is a danger. And the messages Myg sends around the body causes certain things to happen.

So, to shout 'No' at the alien and throw my backpack really hard, I need lots of energy in my body. I need to take deep breaths, and I need strength in my arms.

To run away from the crocodile, I need strength in my legs.

And, because a big purple hairy monster is really scary, Myg shuts everything down so I can hide.

We call these responses:

- *Fight – fighting the alien*
- *Flight – fleeing from the crocodile*
- *Freeze – so still the big purple hairy monster can't see me*

Activity – Appendix 6 (Fight, flight, freeze)

Children can work through this activity individually, in pairs or in small groups, and then share their answers with everyone else. This activity can include all sorts of reasons for the actions. They do not have to be related to fear and anxiety and they do not have to be factual or based in reality. It is to encourage children to think about how they use their bodies – sometimes we choose to shout or run or freeze, but sometimes these things also happen automatically.

Discussion

What else might happen to someone's body if they met an alien or a crocodile?

You are looking for the early warning signs (for more on this, see the resource *Something Has Happened*) and natural, physiological stress responses: jelly legs, feeling sick, wanting the toilet, shaking, gasping for breath, heart beating fast, sweating, not thinking straight ...

For each of these there is a physiological explanation:

- Jelly legs – increased blood flow to the legs, to give them the energy to run, can cause them to feel weak initially.
- Feeling sick – the stomach stops digestion to conserve energy, which is needed by the legs to run.
- Wanting the toilet – the body will get rid of any excess it doesn't need, such as weight from the bladder and bowel.
- Shaking – the muscles are preparing to run or to fight.
- Gasping for breath – the body wants as much air as possible to get oxygen into the bloodstream and around the body.
- Heart beating fast – the heart needs to pump blood around the body, carrying the oxygen needed for energy.
- Sweating – the body's cooling system is preparing for excess heat caused by running or fighting.
- Not thinking straight – the thinking part of the brain, called the prefrontal cortex, is compromised (shut down) by the amygdala.

(There are a few more examples and explanations in Session 3.)

Read pages 13 and 14 of the storybook *Myg and Me*.

Activity

Using **Appendix 7,** the body outline, draw a picture of Myg sending messages around the body and what is happening to the body.

These are all natural feelings, and in the next session we will see that everyone has them.

At the end of this session, allow the children to recover from talking about these fear responses by doing a breathing exercise (see Session 5) or listen to some music, or encourage them to talk about some 'favourite things' – a song, TV programme, video game, pizza …

Session 3
This Happens to Everyone

Anxiety is 'normal'

Recap the previous session.

In the last session we learned how Myg the amygdala sends messages to your body if you are in danger. And we are all really glad that it does, because that helps to keep us alive.

Read pages 15–19 of the storybook *Myg and Me*.

Yes it's great that Myg helps to keep us safe but because it acts so quickly sometimes it decides there is danger without checking it out without taking the time to check if it is really dangerous or just a bit new or different. So, because the amygdala just can't tell the difference between anxiety and danger, it is really useful for us to be able to be in charge at those times – when there isn't a real danger, but it feels like it because we are anxious. And we all feel anxious sometimes. Grown-ups and children. Those feelings we have when we are anxious can be just like the feelings when there is danger, because Myg is making them happen. So we might be feeling uncertain, nervous or anxious, or we might be about to do something new – and our legs might be shaking, we might feel sick, we might want the loo, and those feelings are happening because Myg is thinking 'Danger!!!' But all of these feelings can happen to us when there is no danger. They can happen when we feel nervous or anxious and that is Myg sending messages to our body.

Myg thinks doing a school test is like meeting an alien.

Myg thinks meeting the neighbour's new dog is like meeting a crocodile.

Myg thinks jumping off the diving board is like having a big purple hairy monster at the window. This is when we have to be in charge, so that we can do the test, or meet the dog, or jump off the diving board or any of the other things that make us feel anxious but that we want to do.

And it happens to everyone.

DOI: 10.4324/9781003204459-4

Activity – When might someone feel anxious? (Appendix 8)

All these people will feel anxious at times – when do you think they might feel anxious?

Children can complete the activity sheet, describing things each character on the list of occupations might have to do which may cause them to feel anxious.

Remind them that feeling anxious happens to everyone and that we all might feel differently and that is OK, too. (See the book *Feel, Think and Do with Ruby, Rafa and Riz* for more on this.)

Ideas can then be shared. How many suggestions have they come up with? Look for different suggestions for the same occupation. Which job might be the most 'scary'? Why?

Question: *What do a firefighter, or an astronaut, or a goalie, have to do in order to get their job done?*

Answer: *Be able to calm themselves. Be in charge of their anxieties.*

Activity – What about you? (Appendices 9 and 10)

This activity can be done by individual children or in larger groups or classes. For individuals or small groups, use small continuum cards **(Appendix 9)** laid out on a table and cut up the Anxious? cards **(Appendix 10)** for the child to place on the continuum.

For bigger groups you may wish to enlarge the continuum cards. Lay the cards on the floor in a large space to enable the children to move around and stand by their chosen card. They may choose to stand in between the cards to indicate a less precise description of how they might feel.

Yes – I think I would feel anxious doing this.

Maybe – I might feel a bit unsure, but I'd be OK.

No – I don't think I would feel anxious doing this.

Read out the Anxious? events from **Appendix 10** or make sets of cards to give to small groups to work through. For each event/activity, they will decide where on the continuum they would be. The children should decide for themselves. Encourage them not to just stand with their friends (which they may do initially), but to choose what is true for them.

Allow them to then suggest more events/activities.

A key learning here is that different people will feel differently, and that is OK.

So we know that when we are anxious, Myg starts sending messages around our bodies to prepare us to fight, or to run, or to freeze, just in case it is a dangerous event. The reason we might feel differently to someone else is because we all have our own Myg that responds in its own way.

In Session 2 we talked about some of the ways our bodies respond. There are more ways that we might feel when we are anxious.

Take some more suggestions if they have them, or share the following:

Quick shallow breaths – so I don't waste oxygen.

Feel dizzy – because of the build-up of oxygen in my body and my brain.

Go red/blush – blood rushing to the surface of my skin to cool me down and because my heart is beating fast.

Dry mouth – my body stops producing saliva because it's not needed.

Yawn – a way of getting more oxygen into my body.

Butterflies – my tummy shutting down digestion to save energy.

Another relaxation is a good idea here, after talking about anxiety.

Session 4
Where is My Brilliant Brain?

What happens to my brain when I am anxious?

Read pages 20–22 of the storybook *Myg and Me.*

Activity – What can't I do? (Appendix 11)

What are the things that you might find tricky or difficult to do because Myg is stopping your brilliant brain from working brilliantly?

Using the activity sheet, children can use words or pictures to describe lots of examples of actions that require thinking, remembering and concentration, which are compromised when the amygdala takes charge at times of anxiety.

Discuss the suggestions they have made.

A key causal/maintenance factor of anxiety is predicting the future and predicting catastrophe, the worst that can happen. This will then get in the way of doing the thing we want to do or need to do.

Because our brains are so brilliant, they are able to imagine the future and this can cause anxiety, too. We sometimes imagine the worst thing happening and that can get in the way. So someone might want a part in the school play, but imagining what it would be like to forget all their lines might stop them from taking part.

DOI: 10.4324/9781003204459-5

Discussion

What other examples can you think of – imagining what might happen if …?

Who can remember what we talked about in Session 2 that began with the letters 'f', 'f' and 'f'?

We talked about fight, flight and freeze.

Why did Myg make the body feel like fighting?

To fight the alien.

Why did Myg make the body feel like fleeing/running away?

To get away from the crocodile.

Why did Myg make the body freeze?

To hide from the big purple hairy monster.

But those words – 'fight', 'flight' and 'freeze' – can mean a lot more than fighting, running away and freezing to the spot.

Activity – How might they look? (Appendix 12)

If I am anxious and Myg is in charge, it can look like this.

Draw the first grid from **Appendix 12** on the IWB or flipchart. One at a time, fill in each space, going through each response.

Draw the second grid and ask the children to add more examples of when they might feel anxious.

These are explanations. They are not intended to be excuses for poor behaviour, but they are reasons why a child might struggle. Using this resource with a child or children can be a way, not only to highlight when and why their behaviour or actions may be unpredictable or unacceptable, but crucially to give them strategies to manage troubling feelings and avert or avoid those behaviours and actions.

Read pages 25–28 of the storybook *Myg and Me*.

In our next session, we are going to learn lots of things that you can do to help you to be a Child in Charge.

But before that, and because sometimes we all need a bit of help, we are going to think about how important it is to ask for help if you don't think you can manage your feelings all by yourself.

(If you want to do more on trusted adults and talking about feelings and thoughts, see *Something Has Happened: Supporting Children's Right to Feel Safe* and *Feel, Think and Do with Ruby, Rafa and Riz.*)

It is so important for children to be with an adult who notices, as you can then be the one who says, 'I think you look anxious, worried, upset, unhappy … Is that right?' or to ask, 'What would you like me to do? What can I do to help? Is there anything you want to tell me?' And then, 'It sounds like you are anxious – that's OK, let's see what we can do.'

But sometimes we may not notice as quickly as we would hope to, so giving a child an easier 'in' to speak with us can be helpful.

A trusted person is someone you feel really safe with. Someone who will listen to you, who is on your side, who won't hurt you. I would like to be that trusted person for you. That means, if you are feeling very anxious, or have a worry that feels really big and don't think you can be in charge, you can tell me about it and I will help you. Sometimes you will feel able to come and tell me, and sometimes you might not know what to say. If you don't know what to say, you can let me know by using your 'Can I talk to you?' card (see Activity box below).

Activity – My 'Can I talk to you?' card (Appendix 13)

Each child makes a card with their name on the back.

They can put it on your table or desk, or hand it to you. Or they can put it out on their table or desk for you to see.

Extra guidance

Responding to and supporting a child

This guidance can also be used in conjunction with Session 5.

Remember you are not protecting them from a real threat but from the feelings, thoughts, physiology and behaviours that come with anxiety. However, there is always the possibility that a child may approach you about a significantly harmful situation. That is when you must respond according to your organisation's safeguarding procedures. Please ensure you know what these procedures are – who your DSL or safeguarding lead is, and that you cannot keep risk of significant harm confidential. (For more on this, please see *Something Has Happened*.)

As I said in the Introduction, anxiety shows up when the thing feels bigger than us. Our perception is, we don't have the capacity to cope with what is being asked of us or what we are asking of ourselves. So, I want to say just a little more about the importance of validation.

Validation is not reassurance. It is about coming into the child's space – mentalising, imagining what it might feel like for them.

'I know this feels big for you' is a simple phrase that can mean so much. 'Big' can mean unmanageable, overwhelming, scary.

Can you think of a time when someone belittled or ridiculed you or simply minimised a fear or worry you have had? How did that feel? I would guess that you may have felt unheard, not taken seriously, that they had no idea, didn't understand, didn't get it.

'I know this feels big for you' can help the child to see that you get it. And, as a consequence, they are more likely to trust you, to go with you, to believe you, to feel OK enough.

Whereas, if we are saying, 'There's nothing to worry about …', then that serves to increase the feelings of anxiety, of unsafeness, because the brain is going, 'Well, they don't see the danger, so they're no help and I'm in even more danger now.'

We can help their amygdala, their brain, to learn that it is safe enough, OK enough, to give them the experience of this big thing being safe enough.

Session 5 will give children some skills and techniques to help them work through their anxiety. But, before that, and if it is something they cannot manage themselves, then we can do things to help them feel connected and supported to take on those feelings and thoughts.

We know that fight, flight and freeze can appear in different ways, and some of these may include extreme behaviours and actions.

What can we do to counteract and calm that response?

Key to success here is awareness that we, ourselves, may be in fight or flight mode as well as the child. If we are dealing with a child who is not able to control themselves, it may be alarming to us. So, remaining calm and professionally detached is not natural here. It may feel counterintuitive – that it is contradicting our own fight/flight response. Demonstrate calm, and try to model a calm and measured response.

We know that children are good at noticing when others around them are anxious and will watch the behaviour of others to work out whether they, too, should feel anxious themselves. Even if you're feeling anxious on the inside, you can help the child by remaining calm on the outside. This will help to reassure them that things might be difficult, but they are manageable. We need the skills of self-regulation ourselves in order to:

- counteract our natural flight/flight response
- recognise that trying to reason with an angry, frightened child is not easy and may not be helpful
- recognise signs
- intervene early
- reduce level of agitation.

The adult needs to notice their own physiological responses and manage them.

Fight – a child in fight is ready to do battle

Matching – if you are too calm, the psychological distance between them and you may be too far.

Match the child's energy (not their behaviour) – to contain the child we need to match their energy levels. If there is too much distance between what they are experiencing and how we come across to them, it can be difficult to meet and contain them. This doesn't mean we go into fight mode, but that we are not too calm and relaxed. This can look like we don't care, don't empathise, that their feelings don't matter. So we can move our energy up to meet them and then work to bring their energy down with us.

Inclusive language: 'Shall *we* sit down over here?', 'Shall *we* go for a walk outside?', '*I* can see *you* are upset/angry/frightened …', 'It is OK with *me* for *you* to be anxious/scared/angry …'

Connect and mentalise before exploring the consequences of their behaviour. The fight response in a child can provoke a similar response in an adult – the child shouts, the adult shouts … and this can lead to escalation. Mentalising means thinking about the child's experience.

Expect and accept that they may not understand their behaviour. Asking them 'Why did you do that?' may not help. (See *Feel, Think and do with Ruby Rafa and Riz* for more on managing behaviour.)

An active calming activity – jumping jacks, running around outside/in the playground.

Deep breathing – it's not the time to start to teach them breathing techniques (the amygdala will have them in shallow, gasping breathing), so we need to do this at a time when the child is calm and relaxed, feeling safe, feeling OK. That is when we teach the strategies (Session 5). However, you can say, 'Blow your worried/angry/scared feelings out of your mouth, breathe in calm air through your nose', to encourage them to slow down and calm their breathing.

Flight – a child in flight is ready to run

Stay close to the child.

Give them an easy and familiar task to do.

Have a safe place for them to go – somewhere accessible and allowed.

Allow/enable them to have a comforter.

Gently talk through what they are struggling with.

Speak to the group rather than the child as an individual.

Freeze – a child in freeze has lost connection

Tell them they are OK and safe.

Remind them you are here with them.

Gently remind the child where they are.

Give them smaller tasks, more contained tasks.

Physical contact where appropriate and acceptable for the child – a hand on the shoulder.

Sensory activity – play dough, sand play.

Session 5 will add to all of the above.

Always remember:

Anxiety is not the enemy, but it does have power and sometimes that can overwhelm us.

The more we can understand it, the more we know about it, and then the more power we can have over it. And, if we can recognise the anxiety, accept it, let it happen, be in charge, then we are telling our brains that there isn't a threat.

Put your worries in my pocket

If a child comes to you with a worry, offer to do the worrying for them. Write down the worry on a piece of paper, fold it up and put it in your pocket. You will then keep that worry for the day so that they don't have it and if they want it back at the end of the day, they can come and ask for it. If the worry is a safeguarding issue you would follow your settings safeguarding procedures instead.

Session 5
Lots of Ways to Help

A wide variety of self-calming activities and strategies, using all of the senses

As this session contains all self-calming, self-regulation activities and strategies, the Activity box outline has not been used.

The strategies have been grouped into different areas and different types, and it is important that children experience a range (if not all), so that they can decide what works for them.

You will control how much time you take with these.

You may want to deliver these as a continuation of the sessions already delivered – as shorter, 'drop-in' sessions at the start or end of each day (for schools), as part of an 'off-timetable' day (for schools) or as part of a longer, personalised session with an individual child.

In Session 6, the children will choose up to five strategies they feel comfortable with, which work for them and they can access easily. They will then create their own Child in Charge cards.

Encourage the children to think about when they may need to use their chosen strategies – for example:

- at the start of each day
- before a particular event
- preparing for a test
- attempting something new
- making a new friend
- answering a question in class
- reading aloud.

DOI: 10.4324/9781003204459-6

We know that Myg sometimes prepares for danger when there isn't one there, but when we are a bit uncertain, nervous or unsure.

This is when we need to take control and say, 'Hey Myg, I'm OK. I can do this.'

Taking control means doing something. Perhaps doing something different to what you have done before. So now we are going to learn lots of different things that we can try, to let Myg know that we are in control.

Positive self-talk

'It's not what we say out loud … it's what we whisper to ourselves.' (Robert T. Kiyosaki)

It is easy to forget that we all have an unfiltered, unregulated, uncontrolled voice in our heads. Unfortunately, that voice is not always helpful. It tells us lies, it puts us down, it criticises and admonishes us. It is just the same for both adults and children, but that is a whole other book in itself … For the moment, how can we help children to challenge that negative self-talk, which can increase anxiety?

We all have an inside voice, a voice in our heads – our thoughts. Sometimes these thoughts help us (for example, when we are trying to work something out), and sometimes they don't help us at all.

Your inside voice – your thoughts, the voice in your mind – says things that you don't necessarily say out loud. Often this inside voice happens without you even realising it, but what you say in your mind can affect how you feel about yourself. Do you notice what your inside voice is saying?

It is a good idea to try and get better doing this, because if you notice and it isn't helping, then you can do something about it.

So:

Notice your inside voice.

Is it helping you or not?

Can it help you more?

Practise changing it.

I can do this (Appendix 14)

Fifteen positive 'inside voice' phrases that children can think about, discuss and choose to use.

Encourage the child to think of their own phrases, too, and to keep their inside voice in the present (not the past or the future).

They can choose their top five favourite phrases and make their own cards. These can be kept in their pocket, pencil case, folder, drawer or eventually put with their Child in Charge cards.

And breathe …

When we are anxious, our breathing sometimes gets quicker and shallower. Slowing our breathing down and taking deeper breaths can fool our brains (especially Myg) into thinking that we are relaxed!

And, if our brain thinks we are relaxed, we can become relaxed.

Here are two simple breathing exercises:

Hot chocolate breathing

Imagine you have a mug of lovely hot chocolate in your hands.

Breathe in deeply through your nose, as if you are smelling the chocolatey smell, for a count of 3.

Then breathe out through your mouth, as though you are blowing to cool down the hot chocolate, for a count of 3.

Repeat, but this time try cooling it down for a count of 4.

Then for a count of 5.

And then for a count of 6.

The longer you breathe out, the better.

Blowing bubbles

Imagine you have a tube of bubble mixture (or really use one!).

While you dip the wand into the mixture, breathe in through your nose for a count of 4.

Then blow the bubbles for a count of 4.

Breathe in for a count of 4.

Then blow for a count of 5.

Breathe in for a count of 4.

Then blow for a count of 6.

The longer you blow out, the better.

Relaxation

A quick relaxation that can be done in seconds is to stretch like a cat.

Stretch everything – arms, legs, face, neck, fingers, mouth – and then flop.

Now you are ready to work, or to play, or to chat, or whatever you need to do.

Or there is the melting iceberg.

Do you remember reading about freezing to the spot on the top diving board?

Another good way to relax is to imagine being frozen solid, just like an iceberg, and then slowly melting … melting … melting.

If you have more time:

Tense and relax

This can be done sitting in a chair, but ideally lying comfortably on the floor.

Close or lower your eyes.

Listen to your breathing – in through the nose, out through the mouth – just like with 'Hot chocolate breathing' or 'Blowing bubbles' (see above).

Notice your breathing. What is happening to your body? Is your chest going up and down? Is your tummy going up and down?

Now scrunch up your toes as tight as you can … and relax.

Repeat.

Now tighten the muscles in your legs … and relax.

Repeat.

Now tighten the muscles in your bottom … and relax.

Repeat.

Now tighten your fingers into a fist … and relax.

Repeat.

Now tighten your arms and lift your shoulders up to your ears … and relax.

Repeat.

Now screw up your face really tight … and relax.

Repeat.

Now you are going to do all of those at the same time.

Toes, legs, bottom, fingers, arms, shoulders, face … and relax.

You're going to do it again and this time notice how your body feels when you relax.

Does it feel heavy? Do you feel like you're sinking into the floor, or into your chair?

Relax and notice your breathing again.

Stay relaxed, noticing your breathing.

When you are ready, stretch like a cat, open your eyes, slowly sit up (if lying down) and smile at the person next to you.

Now you are ready.

Visualisation

The relaxation described above can also be followed with this visualisation after the final relax. Do it while the children are still lying or sitting with their eyes closed (preferably, but only if they feel safe to do so) or lowered. Take your time and move slowly through this exercise.

Continue to notice your breathing.

And to notice what is happening to your body.

Now imagine/make a picture in your mind of a lovely place.

This can be a real place or an imaginary one. You can choose:

- *a place where you would like to be*
- *a place where you feel comfortable*
- *a place where you feel safe; your perfect place.*

Pause.

Look around your perfect place and notice what you can see.

What is there? (Don't speak out loud – just use your inside voice.)

Pause.

What sounds can you hear in your perfect place? Or what sounds might you like to hear?

Pause.

Is there a scent or smell or perfume in your perfect place?

Pause.

Is there a taste in your perfect place? Is there something you would like to taste there?

Pause.

If you reached out your hand, what would you feel or touch in your perfect place?

Pause.

How does your body feel in your perfect place?

Pause.

Keeping your eyes closed or lowered, bring your mind back to where we are. Notice the sounds you can hear in this room or in the distance.

Pause.

Now see how quickly your mind can go back to your perfect place – the sights, sounds, smells, tastes and feelings.

Try to use all of your senses if you can. It's OK if you can only use one or two.

Enjoy your perfect place and remember you can always come back here in your mind whenever you want to. It might help you and your Myg to relax.

Pause.

You are going to leave your perfect place now, but it will always be there in your mind so you can go back to it when you need to relax or self-calm.

When you are ready, stretch like a cat, open your eyes, slowly sit up and smile at the person next to you.

Now you are ready.

As a follow-up activity to the visualisation, think about all the different sensations the children experienced using their six senses. What did they see, hear, smell, taste, touch, and how did they feel. This can be done in groups, pairs or individually, and as a drawing, collage or piece of writing.

More quiet, peaceful activities to focus the mind

- colouring in a pattern book
- tracing a simple bold design or figure
- sorting blocks into shapes or colours
- sorting crayons into colours or lengths
- reading a favourite story
- looking at a favourite picture book.

Cosy corner/safe space

Is there a space in your room to set up a cosy corner or safe space? Perhaps add cushions, a soft blanket, a dimmer light than in the rest of the room, soothing scraps (different pieces of fabric – velvet, fur – for stroking), a peaceful pal (soft toy for holding or cuddling).

Can this space be used by a child when they need to calm themselves?

Sensory

These calming strategies use a range of the senses.

Making a pizza

Use the palm of one hand to represent the pizza base. With the other hand, create the pizza toppings. Here are some ideas to start with:

- *Tomato paste – gently sweep the hand back and forward across the 'pizza base'.*
- *Cheese – use the tips of the fingers to gently tap all over the 'pizza base'.*
- *Peppers – use the index finger to pat the 'pizza base'.*
- *Pepperoni – use the index finger to trace small circles on the 'pizza base'.*

Now invent some 'toppings' of your own.

This is a quick strategy that children can try – using their fingers on their hands, making slight, gentle, tickling sensations, can help to reconnect them to their body.

Sensory toy, breathing buddy, peaceful pal, chillin' chum

Having access to a soft toy can help to calm and reassure a child. This could be small enough to be kept in a pocket so that a child can sense it and access it quickly, easily and unobtrusively, or a larger toy that can be kept in sight, which the child is able to cuddle or hold if necessary. It may be a toy given to them by someone they love and feel safe with, or they may have another reason for choosing it.

Other sensory strategies

- Play dough/modelling clay – a sensory experience which many children enjoy. There will be children who won't like this sensation, however.
- Drink a glass of water. Slowly.
- Blow some bubbles. Combine this with the breathing exercise described above ('Blowing bubbles').

Smells

If you use an aroma modelling dough (see 'Other sensory strategies' above), the smell will stay on the hands and can serve as an extra sensory calming strategy.

A child may have a favourite smell – a soap, perfume, scented hand cream, for example – that they associate with being safe and calm (see 'Visualisation' above). Having that smell on a small piece of cloth can be a comfort.

Sounds

There are many sounds that can be calming. Children will also be able to tell you what other sounds they like (see 'Visualisation' above). Here are a few suggestions:

- Indian bells
- wind chimes
- seashell to the ear
- pan pipes
- wind in the trees

- birdsong
- waves
- water bubbling
- cat purring.

Music

Choose a song or piece of music that a child knows and loves.

You may already know of some calming music. If not, try Brian Eno's 'Deep Blue Day' or 'New Space Music'.

Sounds and pieces of music can be downloaded on to an electronic device that the child can access.

Playing a musical instrument can help a child to self-regulate. It can also support a child to feel in control and encourage regulated breathing.

Songs

To the tune of 'If You're Happy and You Know It', try this version to remind children to use their positive inside voice:

If you're anxious and you know it, use your words

If you're anxious and you know it, use your words

If you're anxious and you know it

Then your body's going to show it

If you're anxious and you know it, use your words

If you're worried and you know it, tell someone …

If you're nervous and you know it, take a breath …

If you're wobbly and you know it, use your cards … [when they have made their Child in Charge cards]

Active

Physical activity is helpful in a number of ways. It releases chemicals in the body called endorphins, which can trigger a positive feeling in the body. It can also use up energy in a positive way, and can release anger and frustration safely.

- Dancing – in a large space, with loud music, freestyle.
- Drumming – boxes, saucepans, tabletops will also do if you don't have access to drums. The more noise, fun and laughter, the better.
- Marching – around the building, outside, in a group or alone. Stamping the feet can help to release energy and tension, and can help to reconnect.
- Kicking a ball – a child can kick in a safe, non-harmful way.
- Running, jumping, skipping – simple and easy.

Walking

Going outside can be helpful for some children. Perhaps with an adult they trust, to talk if they want to. It can be beneficial being able to leave the more formal confines of a room/activity, which may be the trigger for their anxiety.

Gardening

If you have a space for a small plot or raised bed where flowers and vegetables can be planted and tended, this can provide longer-term strategies of caring for something, watching it grow and (possibly) eventually eating it, as well as shorter, quicker strategies of 10 minutes outside to water or weed the plants.

Creating

- Painting – big, messy painting can release some frustration. Smaller, careful, more gentle brushstrokes can help to calm.
- Colouring – focusing on an intricate pattern can help to take the child's mind away from an anxiety and can act as a distraction.
- Play dough – as well as being a sensory experience, this can be a creating strategy. Make the longest wiggly worm, or the thinnest wiggly worm, or make a play dough pizza ...

Session 6
Being a Child in Charge

The practice of self-calming

Activity – Creating a set of Child in Charge cards

Once you have explored all the strategies (or as many as you have time for) with the children, they will now be in a position to choose what works for them and to choose a number of personal, individual strategies. Each child can now produce a set of cards to illustrate their chosen approaches to self-calming. If possible, provide them with a small box. An empty matchbox is ideal, with a number of small pieces of card to fit into the box.

Each child chooses a selection of calming strategies that suit them best – from different areas if possible. Five is ideal, but two or three is fine. They can draw on a piece of the card or find a picture that represents the calming strategy.

There are some starter examples of Child in Charge cards in Appendix 15.

The box can then be kept somewhere safe, discreet and accessible, so the child may use it if they feel anxious and need help to calm themselves. The child can choose to get rid of and replace any card that doesn't do the job!

It is important that children learn when and how to use their Child in Charge cards. For example, marching may not be suitable for a busy classroom, but be ideal for the playground or in an individual session. And a relaxation followed by a good stretch may be a great way to start the day for everyone.

There may be some children who will need to use their Child in Charge cards more than others and that process might need to be negotiated and allowed within the setting. Children must know they have permission to use them.

These cards are very useful to share with parents, as they can also be used and practised at home.

DOI: 10.4324/9781003204459-7

Discussion

When everyone has made a set of Child in Charge cards, or at least made a start, encourage the children to talk about which strategies they have chosen, and why.

It is important to emphasise that there is nothing to be self-conscious about needing these cards. You are the ideal model, so make a set for yourself and be honest about how there are times when you need to self-calm, too. Some of the strategies are unobtrusive – making a pizza, breathing, a small breathing buddy (sensory toy), visualising – and children should be encouraged to have at least one of these, as they are something children can use if they don't want to draw attention to themselves.

The more familiar children are with having and using these cards, the easier it will be to refer to them when talking with a child. For instance, 'I can see you are worried about this. What would you like me to do?' 'How can I help you?' or 'Let's use your Child in Charge cards.'

Child in Charge Certificate (Appendix 16)

It is up to you when you award these certificates.

The idea is that they are given to children who have successfully used their calming strategies. This is an ideal opportunity to include home and parents/carers. A child self-calming at home can get a certificate, as well. It is also important to let a child know that by asking a trusted adult for help they are being in charge.

So, to return to the beginning. It may be that you work mainly with children who are significantly anxious, or perhaps you work with groups or classes of children whose experiences and feelings cover a wide range. Or possibly you live with a child who is struggling at the moment. Whichever child or children you work or live with, I hope you have found something in this resource to make their lives feel a little more manageable, so they may feel a little more in control. And maybe you, too, have found a way to manage an anxiety, because it happens to us all.

Appendix 1: My Brilliant Brain

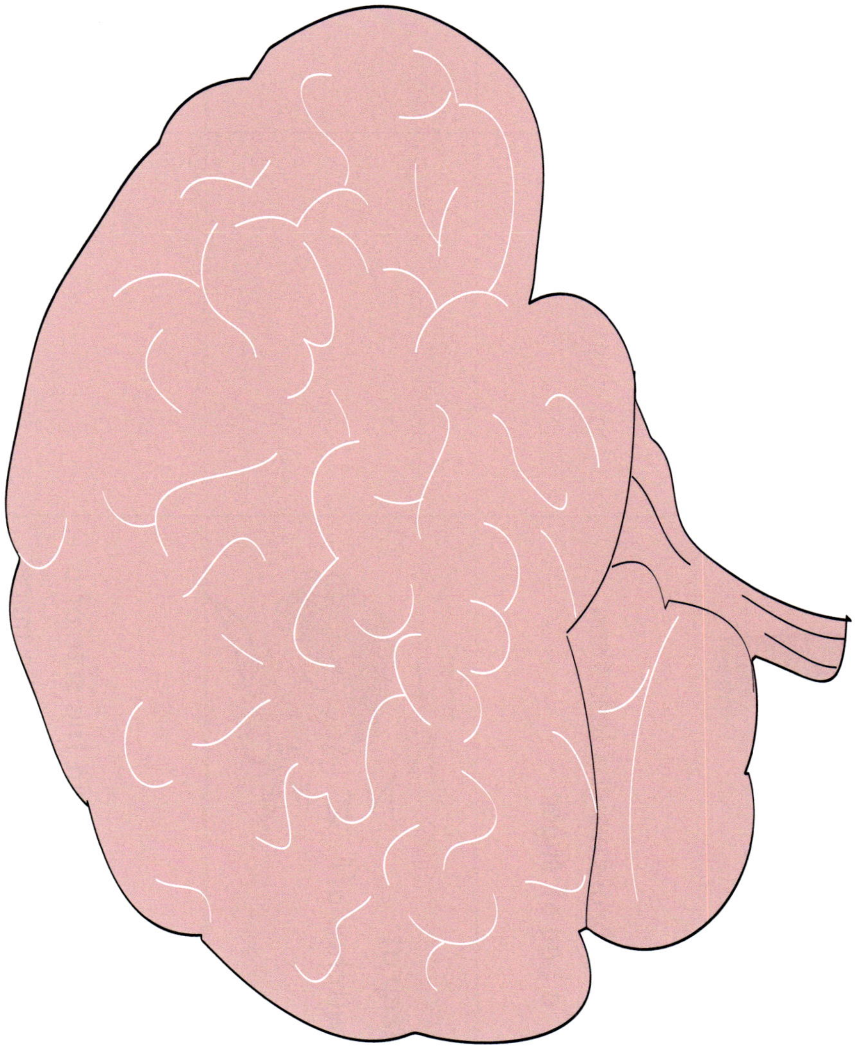

Copyright material from [Bates (2022), *My Brilliant Brain*, Routledge]

Appendix 2: Facts and Fibs

	Fact	Fib
The first human brain transplant was carried out 10 years ago. 		
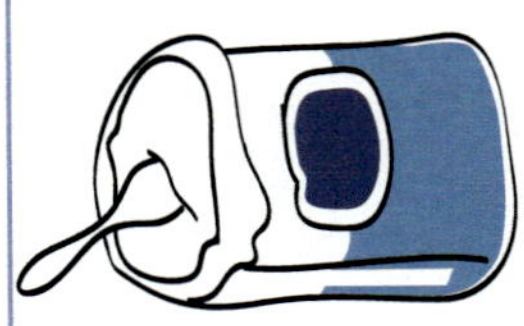 Your brain weighs less than a bag of sugar		
When you go to sleep at night your brain switches off to have a rest 		
 A piece of brain the size of a grain of sand will have more than 100,000 cells		
Information can move around your brain at more than 250 miles an hour (faster that an F1 racing car) or 120 metres a second 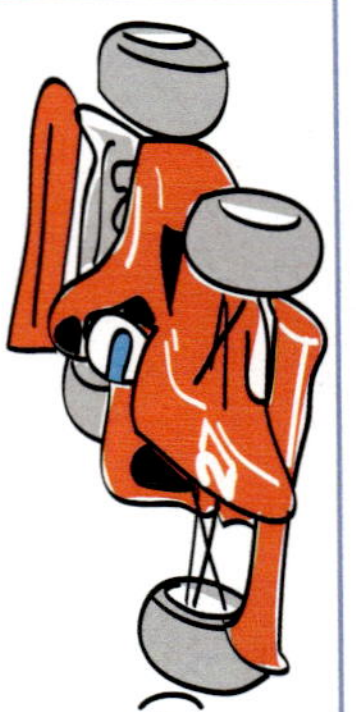		

Copyright material from [Bates (2022), *My Brilliant Brain*, Routledge]

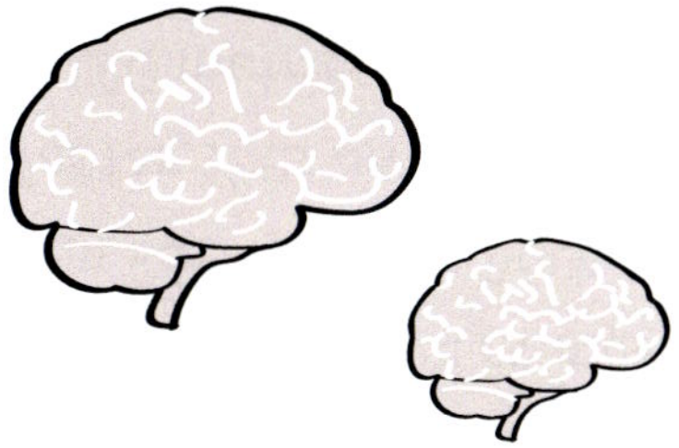 An adult brain has more connections than a 2 year old's brain.		
Your brain has about 1000 thoughts a day 		
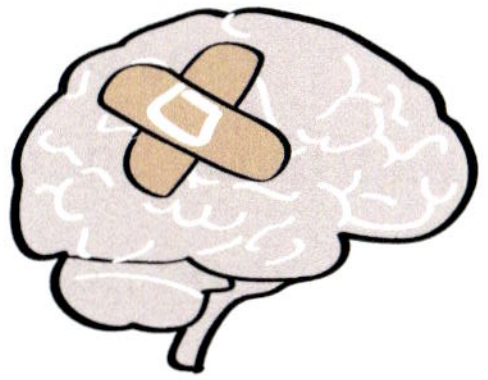 Your brain feels no pain		
Laughing at a joke takes 5 parts of the brain 		
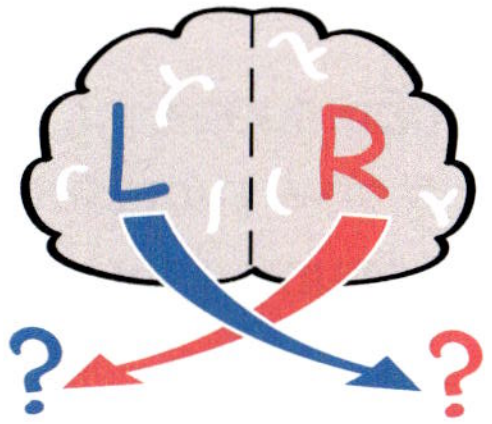 The left side of your brain controls the right side of your body' and the right side controls the left!'		

Copyright material from [Bates (2022), *My Brilliant Brain*, Routledge]

Appendix 3: Facts and Fibs Answers

	Fact	Fib
The first human brain transplant was carried out 10 years ago. 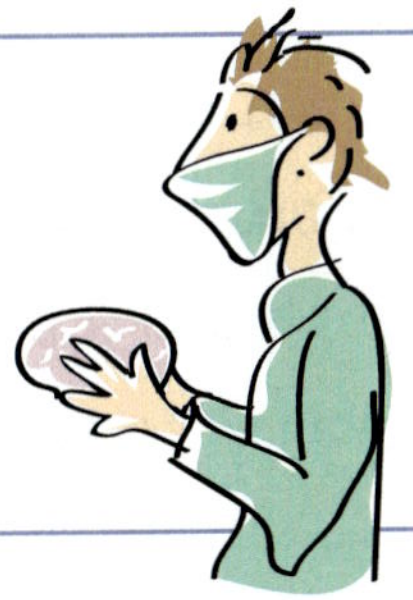		There has never been a human brain transplant
 Your brain weighs less than a bag of sugar	✓	
When you go to sleep at night your brain switches off to have a rest 		Your brain is just as busy when you are asleep...if not more
 A piece of brain the size of a grain of sand will have more than 100,000 cells	✓	
Information can move around your brain at more than 250 miles an hour (faster that an F1 racing car) or 120 metres a second 	✓	

Copyright material from [Bates (2022), *My Brilliant Brain*, Routledge]

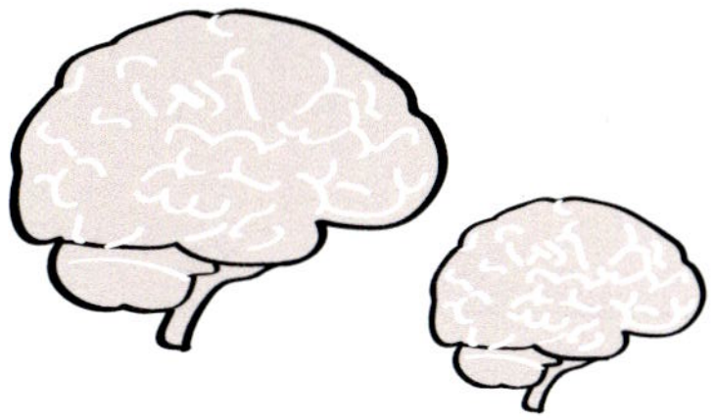 An adult brain has more connections than a 2 year old's brain.		False. A 2 year old's brain has trillions of connections and many of them that will have stopped working by the time they are an adult.
Your brain has about 1000 thoughts a day 		It's more like 50,000!
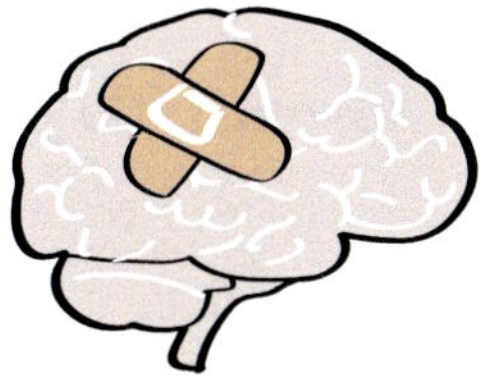 Your brain feels no pain	✓	
Laughing at a joke takes 5 parts of the brain 	✓	
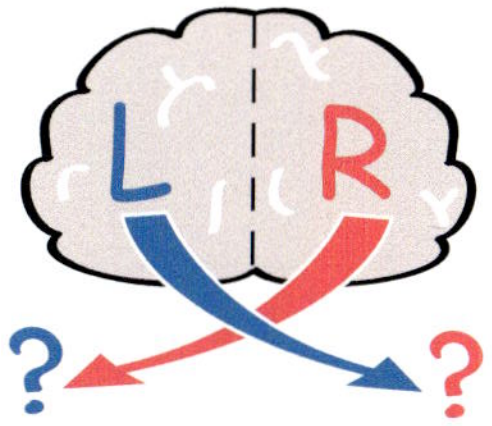 The left side of your brain controls the right side of your body' and the right side controls the left!'	✓	

Copyright material from [Bates (2022), *My Brilliant Brain*, Routledge]

Appendix 4: Where in the Brain...?

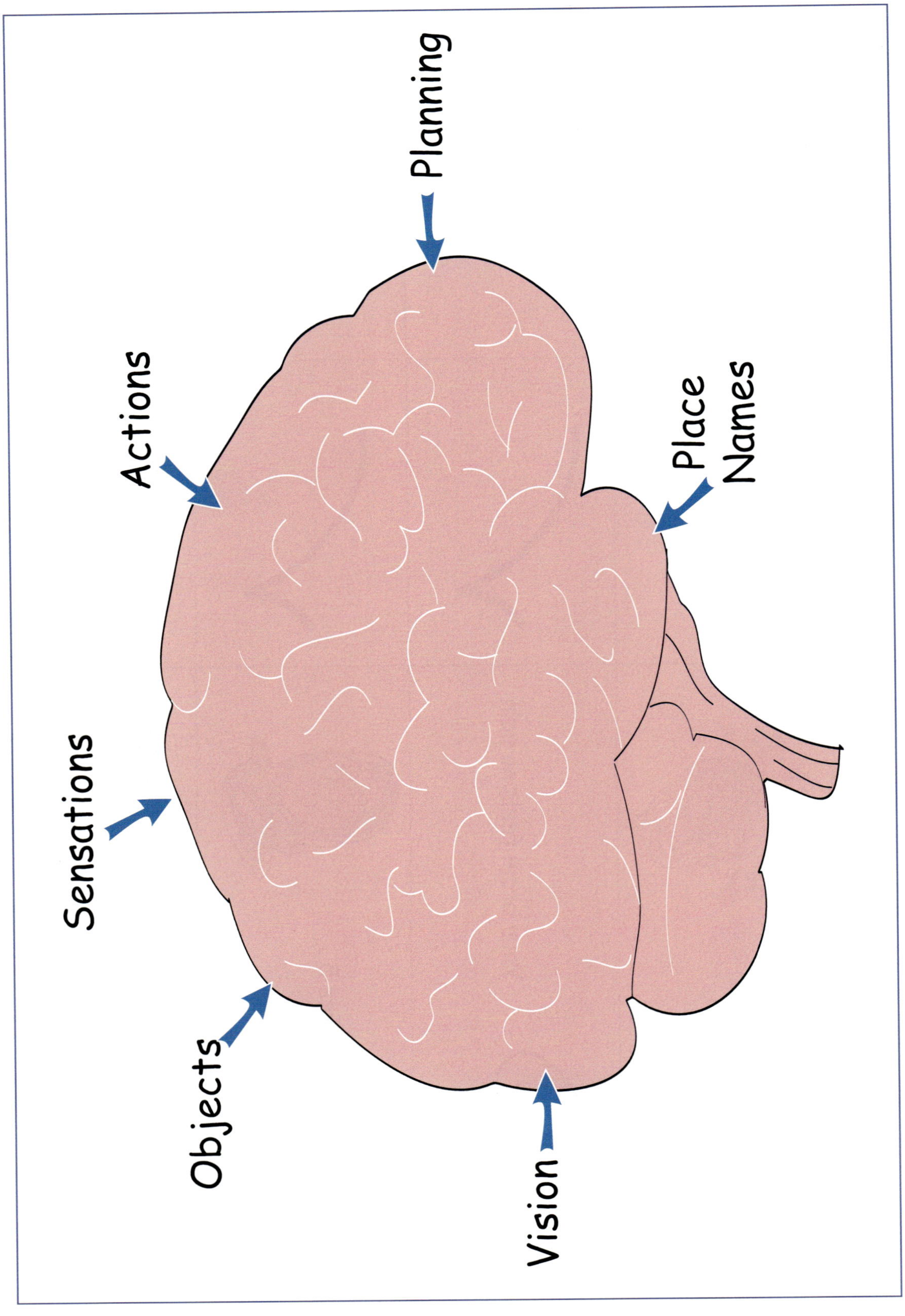

Copyright material from [Bates (2022), *My Brilliant Brain*, Routledge]

Appendix 5: Here is the Amygdala

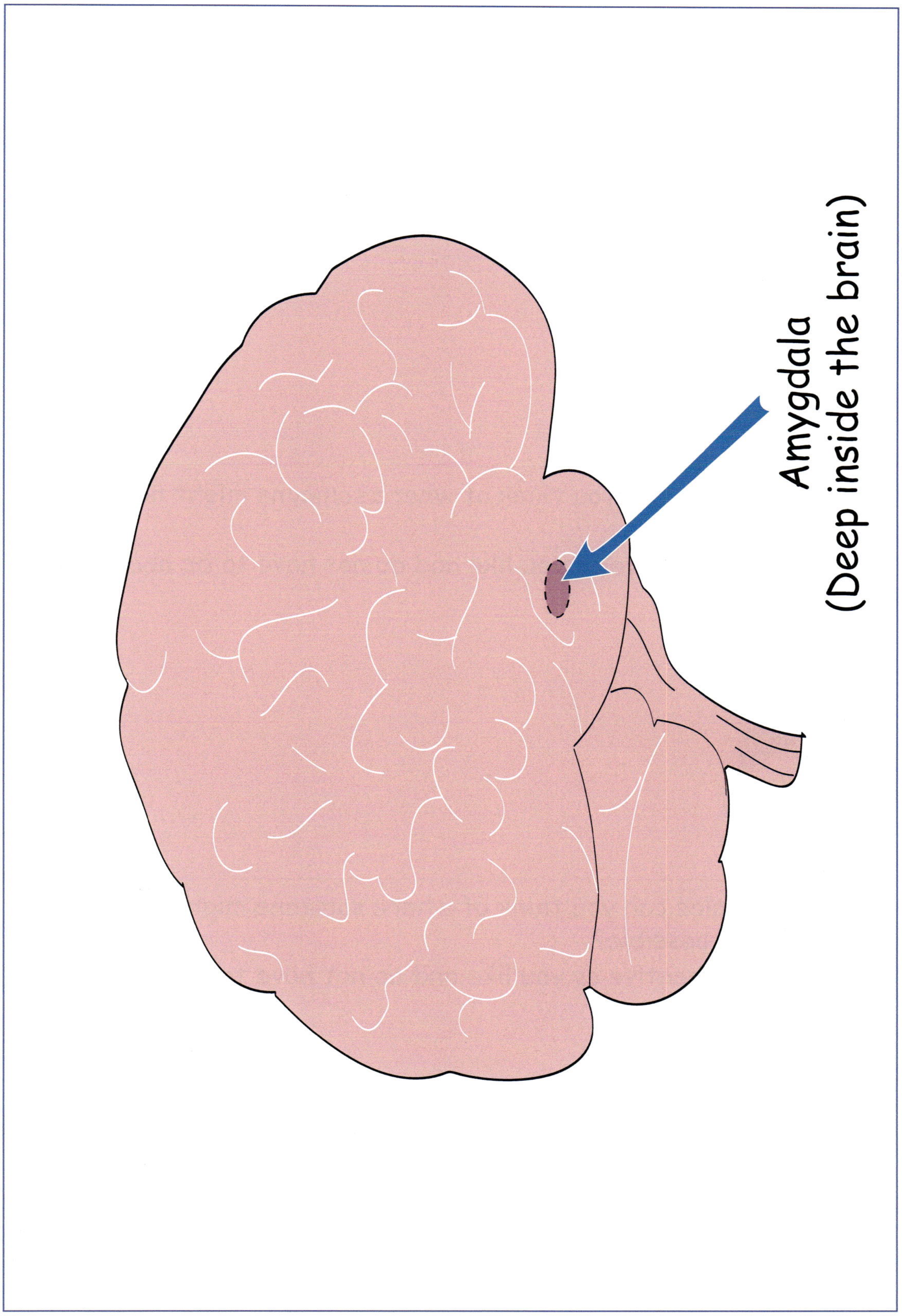

Copyright material from [Bates (2022), *My Brilliant Brain*, Routledge]

Appendix 6: Fight, Flight and Freeze

How many examples can you think of where someone might have to shout at the top of their voice?

These can be as creative as you like and do not have to be about real life.

How many examples can you think of where someone might need to run really fast?

These can be as creative as you like and do not have to be about real life.

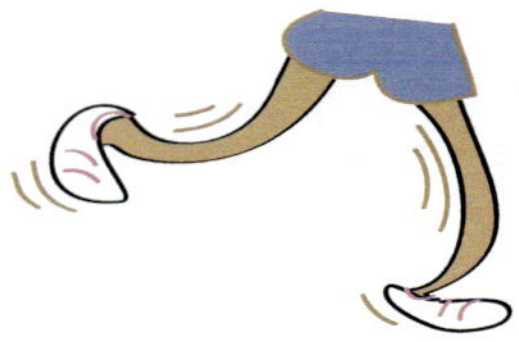

How many examples can you think of where someone might need to be as still and quiet as possible?

These can be as creative as you like and do not have to be about real life.

Copyright material from [Bates (2022), *My Brilliant Brain*, Routledge]

Appendix 7: Body Outline

Copyright material from [Bates (2022), *My Brilliant Brain*, Routledge]

Appendix 8: When Might Someone Feel Anxious?

Chef 	
Celebrity 	
Footballer 	
Astronaut 	
Teacher 	
Builder 	
Firefighter 	
Vet 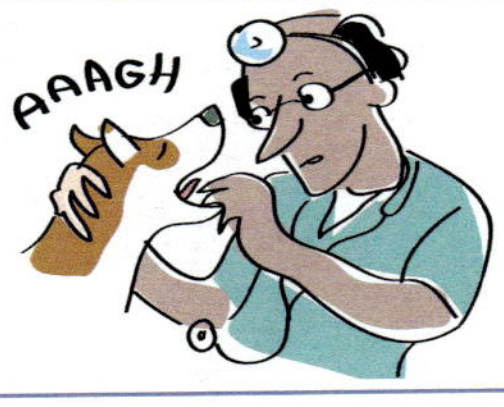	

Copyright material from [Bates (2022), *My Brilliant Brain*, Routledge]

Appendix 9: Yes, No, Maybe

YES

NO

MAYBE

Copyright material from [Bates (2022), *My Brilliant Brain*, Routledge]

Appendix 10: Anxious?

Climbing high on a climbing frame 	Going to a party 
 Making a cake	Doing my homework 
Being late for school 	Singing in the choir 
Playing a computer game 	 Speaking in assembly
 Sleeping at my friend's house	Going to secondary school 

Copyright material from [Bates (2022), *My Brilliant Brain*, Routledge]

Appendix 11: What Can't I Do?

What are the things that Myg might stop you from doing because Myg is stopping your brilliant brain from working brilliantly.

Remembering my times tables 	Playing my computer games 

Copyright material from [Bates (2022), *My Brilliant Brain*, Routledge]

Appendix 12: FFF – How Might They Look?

Fight	*Flight*	*Freeze*
Hot and bothered	Being silly	Confused
Angry	Not sitting still	Forgetful
Shouting	Not doing my work	Not listening
Being mean to my friends	Finding excuses	Daydreaming
Being rude	Running away	Unfinished work

And this is because I feel anxious about:

Getting it wrong
Being left out
Making a mistake
Not being liked
Finding something hard to do
Being different

Copyright material from [Bates (2022), *My Brilliant Brain*, Routledge]

Appendix 13: 'Can I Talk to You?'

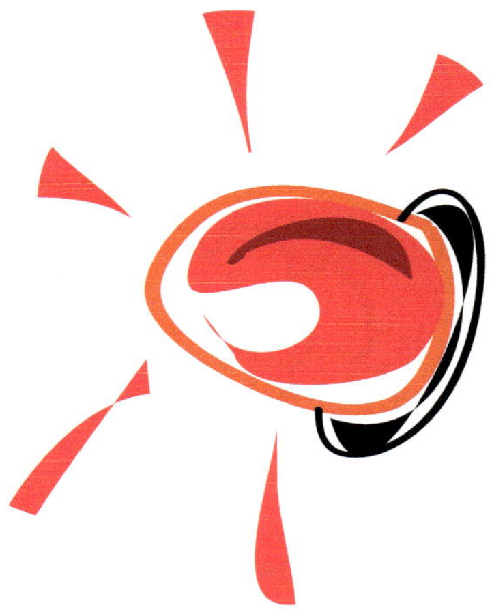

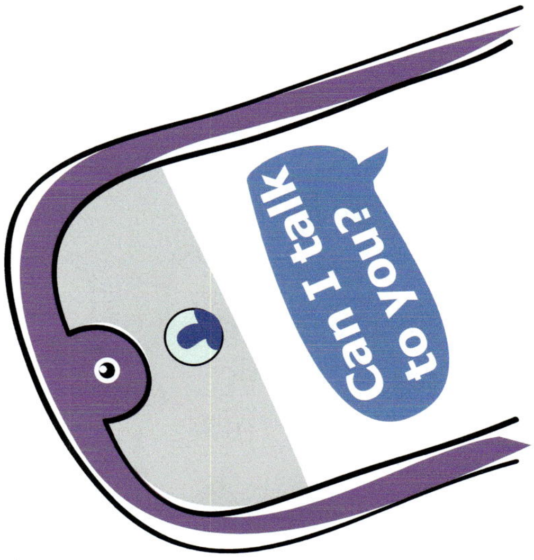

Copyright material from [Bates (2022), *My Brilliant Brain*, Routledge]

Appendix 14: I Can Do This

I can do this	I really want to try it	I've got this
This is hard, but I think I can do this	I don't have to be perfect, no-one else is	I can ask for help
It's OK	I can have a go	I know how to relax
Things are getting better	It's ok if I get it wrong	It's ok to ask for help
It's scary but I am safe	It can be fun to feel scared	I can always try again

Copyright material from [Bates (2022), *My Brilliant Brain*, Routledge]

Appendix 15: Child in Charge Cards

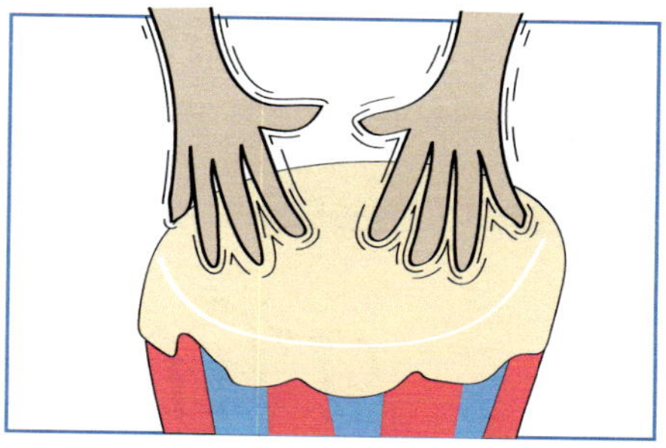

Copyright material from [Bates (2022), *My Brilliant Brain*, Routledge]

Appendix 16: Child in Charge Certificate

This is to certify

- - - - - - - - - - - - - - - - - -

is a

Child In Charge !

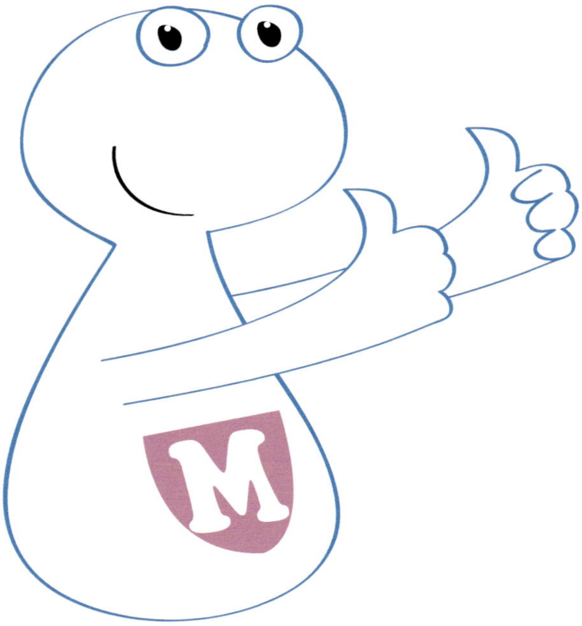

Copyright material from [Bates (2022), *My Brilliant Brain*, Routledge]